Foreword

Introduction

This eBook is the TENTH in the series, and the focus is **The Future of Industrial Automation: Top 5 Trends for 2030**

Industrial automation is evolving at an unprecedented pace, driven by breakthrough technologies that promise to redefine manufacturing, logistics, and smart infrastructure. The Future of Industrial Automation: Trends and Innovations explores the next decade of industrial evolution, offering insights into game-changing advancements such as blockchain, 5G, quantum computing, and autonomous systems.

This book provides a forward-looking perspective on how AI, automation, and robotics will transform the workforce and industrial landscapes. Discover how next-generation manufacturing systems, digital twins, and hyper-customized production will revolutionize industries. Whether you're an industry leader, a forward-thinking professional, or an automation enthusiast, this book equips you with the knowledge to navigate and capitalize on the future of industrial automation.

About the Author

The Author has more than 30+ years of experience in the field of practical applications of Industrial Automation, IoT, MES, Industry Consulting for Manufacturing Organizations.

THE **DIGITAL** ALLCHEMIST

"Digital alchemy" is a state that a business can strive to achieve by using its assets and technology to redesign operations and innovate. This can help a business digitally transform itself.

Copyright © 2024 by Digital allchemist

Table of Contents

Table of Contents

Foreword 1

Introduction 4

Trend #1: AI-Driven Industrial Autonomy 10

Trend #2: The Industrial Metaverse and Digital Twins 14

Trend #3 - Sustainable and Energy-Efficient Automation 41

Trend #4: Hyperconnected Industrial Ecosystems (5G & IIoT) . 56

Trend #5: The Future Workforce in an Automated World 70

Conclusion: The Road Ahead 82

Introduction

Industrial automation is undergoing a rapid transformation driven by advancements in artificial intelligence (AI), the Internet of Things (IoT), and digital transformation. As we approach 2030, automation will no longer be about merely improving efficiency and reducing costs; it will become the backbone of the global industrial landscape. Several factors make 2030 a pivotal year for industrial automation:

- Maturity of Emerging Technologies: By 2030, technologies such as AI, machine learning, digital twins, and quantum computing will be widely adopted, creating a seamless and highly interconnected industrial ecosystem.
- Sustainability Mandates: Governments and industries worldwide will be pushing for net-zero emissions, requiring automation to play a crucial role in optimizing energy use, reducing waste, and improving supply chain sustainability.
- Aging Workforce and Skill Gaps: Many industries will face a significant shortage of skilled labor, making automation indispensable to maintaining productivity.
- 5G and Edge Computing Advancements: With ultra-fast, low-latency communication, industries will operate in real-time, leveraging predictive analytics and AI-driven decision-making more effectively.
- Economic and Geopolitical Factors: As global competition intensifies, nations and corporations will invest heavily in automation to maintain an edge in manufacturing and industrial productivity.

2030 represents a critical juncture where automation will redefine how industries operate, making it essential for businesses to adapt or risk obsolescence.

Automation has come a long way from its early mechanical roots to today's AI-driven smart factories. Understanding this evolution provides insight into the challenges and opportunities that lie ahead.

The Past: The Industrial Revolutions

- First Industrial Revolution (Late 18th to Early 19th Century): Marked by mechanization using steam engines, industrial automation began with simple mechanical devices that replaced manual labor.
- Second Industrial Revolution (Late 19th to Early 20th Century): Introduction of electricity enabled assembly lines and mass production, improving efficiency and scalability.
- Third Industrial Revolution (Mid-20th Century): The rise of computers and early automation, including programmable logic controllers (PLCs) and robotic arms, paved the way for greater precision and control in manufacturing.

The Present: Industry 4.0 and Smart Factories

We are currently in the era of Industry 4.0, characterized by:

- IoT and Smart Sensors: Real-time monitoring and control of industrial processes through connected devices.
- AI and Machine Learning: Advanced analytics and predictive maintenance to minimize downtime.
- Cyber-Physical Systems: Integration of digital and physical processes for better efficiency and automation.
- Cloud Computing and Edge Processing: Data-driven decision-making at unprecedented speeds.

The Future: Industry 5.0 and Beyond

Looking ahead to 2030, the next stage of industrial automation, often referred to as Industry 5.0, will emphasize:

- Human-Machine Collaboration: Robots and AI systems working alongside human workers to enhance efficiency rather than replace jobs entirely.
- Self-Learning Systems: AI models that continuously improve their accuracy and decision-making abilities without human intervention.
- Sustainability-Driven Automation: Technologies designed to optimize energy usage, reduce carbon footprints, and support circular economy principles.
- Hyperconnected Ecosystems: A seamless integration of supply chains, production lines, and logistics, enabled by AI, 5G, and blockchain.

By 2030, industrial automation will no longer be just an efficiency booster but a necessity for survival in an increasingly complex and competitive world.

1.3 Key Drivers Shaping the Next Decade

Several factors will drive the adoption and evolution of industrial automation through 2030. These include technological advancements, economic shifts, environmental concerns, and workforce dynamics.

Technology Acceleration

- AI and Machine Learning: AI-powered automation will be at the core of industrial processes, enabling predictive maintenance, quality control, and autonomous decision-making.
- Quantum Computing: While still in its infancy, quantum computing could revolutionize optimization problems in supply chain management, material science, and real-time analytics.
- 5G and Beyond: High-speed, low-latency communication will make remote monitoring, cloud-based automation, and decentralized manufacturing more viable.

- Digital Twins: Virtual replicas of physical systems will be used to simulate, predict, and optimize industrial operations.

Sustainability and Green Manufacturing

- Energy Optimization: AI-driven energy management will ensure that industrial processes consume minimal power without compromising efficiency.
- Circular Economy Models: Automation will enable waste reduction, material recycling, and closed-loop production systems.
- Regulatory Compliance: Stringent environmental regulations will push companies to adopt automated sustainability solutions.

Workforce Transformation

- Reskilling and Upskilling: Workers will need to adapt to new technologies, necessitating large-scale training and education initiatives.
- Human-AI Collaboration: Machines will handle repetitive tasks, while human workers will focus on decision-making, innovation, and oversight.
- Ethical and Social Considerations: Governments and businesses must address concerns related to job displacement and the ethical use of AI.

Economic and Geopolitical Factors

- Global Supply Chain Disruptions: Automation will mitigate risks by improving supply chain resilience and agility.
- Nearshoring and Regional Manufacturing: With automation reducing labor dependency, companies will shift production closer to demand centers.
- Investment in Automation Technologies: Governments and corporations will increase funding for automation as a strategic priority for economic competitiveness.

AI, IoT, and digital transformation are the three pillars that will define industrial automation by 2030. Their combined impact will revolutionize every aspect of manufacturing and industrial operations.

Artificial Intelligence (AI) in Industrial Automation

AI will drive the next wave of automation by enabling:

- Predictive Maintenance: AI-powered algorithms will analyze machine data to predict failures before they occur, reducing downtime.
- Autonomous Decision-Making: AI will enable machines to self-optimize processes, improving efficiency and output quality.
- Computer Vision: AI-driven vision systems will enhance defect detection and quality control in manufacturing lines.
- Supply Chain Optimization: AI-powered forecasting models will improve inventory management and demand prediction.

Internet of Things (IoT) and Connected Manufacturing

IoT will enhance industrial automation through:

- Real-Time Data Collection: Sensors will monitor machine health, environmental conditions, and operational performance.
- Remote Monitoring and Control: Industrial equipment will be managed remotely, reducing the need for on-site personnel.
- Seamless Communication Between Machines: IoT-enabled devices will ensure smooth coordination between different stages of production.
- Enhanced Safety: Smart sensors will detect potential hazards and ensure workplace safety.

- Cloud and Edge Computing: Faster data processing will enable real-time decision-making without dependence on centralized servers.
- Blockchain for Industrial Security: Secure, tamper-proof ledgers will be used for supply chain transparency and compliance tracking.
- Augmented and Virtual Reality: AR/VR will assist in training, remote maintenance, and troubleshooting of industrial equipment.
- Cybersecurity Enhancements: As connectivity increases, stronger cybersecurity measures will be necessary to protect industrial infrastructure.

Conclusion

As we move towards 2030, industrial automation will be shaped by rapid advancements in AI, IoT, and digital transformation. The next decade will witness a fundamental shift from traditional automation to AI-driven autonomy, sustainability-focused manufacturing, and hyperconnected industrial ecosystems. Organizations that proactively embrace these trends will thrive in the new era of industrial automation.

Trend #1: AI-Driven Industrial Autonomy

As industrial automation continues to evolve, AI-driven autonomy is emerging as the next frontier. Unlike traditional automation, which relies on pre-programmed instructions, autonomous industrial systems leverage artificial intelligence (AI) to make real-time decisions, self-optimize, and adapt to changing conditions without human intervention. By 2030, AI-powered industrial autonomy will redefine manufacturing, logistics, and production processes, bringing unprecedented levels of efficiency, productivity, and resilience to global industries.

2.1 The Shift from Automation to Autonomous Industrial Systems

Industrial automation has come a long way from its early days of mechanized processes and programmable logic controllers (PLCs). The next leap forward is the transition from automation to autonomy. This shift is driven by advancements in AI, machine learning, and real-time data analytics. Autonomous industrial systems differ from traditional automated systems in three key ways:

1. Decision-Making Capability – Unlike conventional automation that follows predefined rules, autonomous systems use AI to make real-time decisions. These systems analyze vast amounts of data, detect patterns, and determine the best course of action without human intervention.

2. Adaptability – Traditional automation is rigid, requiring reprogramming for any process change. Autonomous systems, however, are dynamic and can adjust operations based on environmental conditions, demand fluctuations, and predictive insights.

3. Self-Optimization – AI-driven industrial systems can learn from past performance, optimizing their processes over time. This ability enables continuous improvement in efficiency, cost savings, and productivity.

One real-world example of this shift is seen in fully autonomous warehouses operated by companies like Amazon and Alibaba. These facilities use AI-powered robots to manage inventory, pick and pack products, and optimize logistics routes with minimal human intervention. By 2030, AI-driven autonomy will extend beyond warehouses to factories, energy plants, and even infrastructure maintenance.

2.2 AI-Powered Decision-Making and Self-Optimizing Factories

The factories of the future will be more than just automated— they will be intelligent. AI-powered decision-making will transform manufacturing by enabling factories to self-optimize operations, predict maintenance needs, and dynamically allocate resources.

Key AI Technologies Driving Self-Optimizing Factories:

- Machine Learning Algorithms: AI continuously analyzes production data to detect inefficiencies and recommend improvements.
- Computer Vision: AI-powered cameras and sensors monitor production lines, detecting defects and quality issues in real time.
- Natural Language Processing (NLP): AI-driven chatbots and voice assistants enable seamless interaction between human workers and machines.
- Digital Twins: Virtual replicas of physical factory systems help in predictive analysis and performance optimization.

For example, Siemens' "Factory of the Future" initiative leverages AI-driven automation to optimize production processes, reducing downtime and improving quality control. By 2030, self-optimizing factories will become mainstream, significantly enhancing global manufacturing efficiency.

2.3 Reinforcement Learning for Real-Time Adaptability

Reinforcement learning (RL), a subset of machine learning, plays a crucial role in enabling real-time adaptability in industrial settings. Unlike supervised learning, which requires labeled datasets, reinforcement learning allows AI systems to learn from trial and error, improving performance over time.

How Reinforcement Learning Works in Industrial Automation:

1. Observation: The AI system continuously monitors factory processes, gathering real-time data.
2. Decision-Making: AI makes predictions and takes actions based on current conditions.
3. Feedback Loop: The system evaluates the outcome of its actions and adjusts future decisions accordingly.

A practical example is Google's DeepMind AI, which uses RL to optimize energy consumption in data centers. By learning from past energy usage patterns, the AI system autonomously adjusts cooling and power distribution, reducing energy costs by up to 40%. By 2030, similar RL-based AI solutions will be applied in industrial automation to enhance efficiency, reduce waste, and improve adaptability.

2.4 The Role of AI in Reducing Downtime and Improving Productivity

Downtime is one of the biggest challenges in industrial automation, leading to significant financial losses. AI-driven predictive maintenance and intelligent monitoring systems will play a vital role in minimizing downtime and improving overall productivity.

Key AI Technologies Reducing Downtime:

- Predictive Maintenance: AI algorithms analyze sensor data to predict equipment failures before they happen.
- Automated Troubleshooting: AI-driven diagnostics rapidly identify and resolve machinery issues.
- Remote Monitoring: AI-powered IoT solutions enable real-time equipment monitoring from anywhere.

For example, General Electric (GE) has implemented AI-driven predictive maintenance in its industrial operations, reducing unplanned downtime by 20%. By 2030, AI-driven maintenance solutions will be standard in manufacturing, energy, and logistics sectors, ensuring uninterrupted operations.

By embracing AI-driven industrial autonomy, industries will experience transformative improvements in efficiency, adaptability, and resilience. As AI continues to evolve, businesses must invest in AI-powered solutions to stay competitive in the next era of industrial automation.

Trend #2: The Industrial Metaverse and Digital Twins

3.1 Introduction: The Rise of the Industrial Metaverse

The concept of the industrial metaverse is gaining traction as companies look for ways to integrate virtual environments, AI, and real-time data analytics to enhance industrial automation. By 2030, industries will leverage digital twins, immersive VR/AR technologies, and AI-driven decision-making to improve operational efficiency, predictive maintenance, and workforce collaboration.

Today, companies like Siemens, NVIDIA, Honeywell, and Microsoft are already investing in digital twins and metaverse technologies, recognizing their potential to transform manufacturing, logistics, and energy sectors.

In this chapter, we will explore:

* How digital twins are transforming predictive maintenance and simulation

* The role of VR and AR in smart factories

* AI-driven process optimization in the industrial metaverse

* Human-machine collaboration through immersive technologies

By 2030, the industrial metaverse will redefine productivity, sustainability, and workforce engagement, making it a key trend in industrial automation.

3.2 Digital Twins: The Foundation of the Industrial Metaverse

What Are Digital Twins?

A digital twin is a real-time virtual representation of a physical asset, system, or process that continuously updates using real-world data.

Digital twins enable companies to:

* Predict failures before they occur

* Optimize industrial processes through simulations

* Enhance remote monitoring and predictive maintenance

How Digital Twins Work

A digital twin operates in three key stages:

1. Data Collection: IIoT sensors collect real-time data from industrial assets.
2. Virtual Modeling: AI algorithms create an accurate digital copy of the physical asset.
3. Simulation & Optimization: Engineers run simulations to predict equipment behavior, optimize workflows, and prevent failures.

Real-World Applications of Digital Twins

Predictive Maintenance in Manufacturing

* General Electric (GE) uses digital twins to monitor jet engines and gas turbines. AI analyzes real-time data to predict maintenance needs, reducing repair costs by 40%.

Current Challenges in Predictive Maintenance

Manufacturers face several key challenges when maintaining industrial equipment:

- Unplanned Downtime: Unexpected machine failures lead to significant production losses and increased costs.
- Reactive Maintenance: Traditional maintenance relies on scheduled servicing or responding to failures after they

occur, often leading to unnecessary repairs or missed warning signs.

- Data Overload: Modern industrial systems generate vast amounts of sensor data, but manual analysis is slow and ineffective in detecting subtle failure patterns.
- High Maintenance Costs: Regular inspections and unexpected breakdowns increase operational expenses, impacting profitability.

Solution: Digital Twins for AI-Powered Predictive Maintenance

To address these issues, GE uses digital twin technology to create virtual models of jet engines and gas turbines. These models are continuously updated with real-time IoT sensor data collected from the physical equipment.

Here's how it works:

1. Real-Time Data Collection – Sensors installed on machines capture vibration, temperature, pressure, and operational efficiency data.
2. AI-Powered Analysis – Machine learning algorithms detect anomalies, wear patterns, and early signs of failure.
3. Predictive Insights – The digital twin simulates different operational conditions and predicts when parts will likely fail.
4. Proactive Maintenance – Instead of fixing problems after they occur, engineers receive alerts and recommendations for maintenance, reducing the risk of unexpected breakdowns.

Benefits of Digital Twins in Predictive Maintenance

* 40% Cost Reduction: GE reports 40% lower maintenance costs by eliminating unnecessary repairs and reducing emergency fixes.

* 50% Less Downtime: Predicting failures before they occur minimizes production disruptions, improving overall efficiency.

* Increased Asset Lifespan: Regular monitoring helps extend the lifespan of critical industrial assets by ensuring optimal operation.

By 2030, predictive maintenance powered by digital twins will be standard practice in industrial automation, improving equipment reliability and reducing costs.

Smart Factories and Process Optimization

* Siemens' Digital Twin Factory in Germany uses AI-driven simulations to optimize production lines before making physical changes, increasing efficiency by 20%.

Current Challenges in Smart Manufacturing

- Trial-and-Error Process Optimization: Traditionally, production lines are improved through physical testing, which is expensive and time-consuming.
- Complex Manufacturing Environments: Factories operate with multiple interdependent systems, making real-time process optimization challenging.
- High Operational Costs: Inefficient workflows lead to wasted energy, labor, and materials.

Solution: AI-Powered Digital Twins for Smart Factory Optimization

Siemens' digital twin factory in Germany leverages AI-driven models to test and optimize production line changes in a virtual environment before implementing them physically.

How the system works:

1. Virtual Factory Model – A digital twin mirrors the real factory, simulating machines, workflows, and production sequences.
2. AI-Driven Simulations – AI tests various workflow scenarios to find the most efficient setup.

3. Real-Time Adjustments – If inefficiencies are detected, the system suggests process improvements before real-world deployment.
4. Automated Optimization – Machine learning continuously refines factory operations, ensuring maximum efficiency over time.

Benefits of Digital Twin-Based Smart Factories

* 20% Higher Efficiency: AI-driven optimizations streamline production workflows, reducing delays and inefficiencies.

* Lower Operational Costs: Optimized processes minimize resource wastage, reducing overall expenses.

* Faster Adaptability: Factories can quickly adjust to new product designs or demand fluctuations without disrupting operations.

By 2030, digital twins will enable factories to become self-optimizing, highly efficient, and adaptive, setting new standards in industrial automation.

Supply Chain Resilience

* Unilever uses digital twins to simulate global supply chain disruptions, reducing production bottlenecks and improving delivery times.

Current Challenges in Industrial Supply Chains

- Disruptions from Global Events: Supply chains are vulnerable to natural disasters, geopolitical tensions, and pandemics.
- Demand Fluctuations: Companies struggle to balance inventory levels with changing customer demands.
- Logistical Complexities: Coordinating global suppliers, manufacturing plants, and distributors is challenging.

Solution: Digital Twins for Supply Chain Optimization

Unilever has developed a supply chain digital twin that enables real-time simulation of global logistics and inventory flows.

How it works:

1. Real-Time Data Integration – The system aggregates supplier, transportation, and warehouse data.
2. Scenario Analysis – AI-driven models test "what-if" scenarios to predict disruptions and their impact.
3. Proactive Adjustments – If risks are detected, Unilever can shift suppliers, adjust production levels, or reroute logistics before disruptions occur.

Benefits of Digital Twins in Supply Chains

* Fewer Bottlenecks: AI-driven optimizations prevent supply chain delays, ensuring consistent production.

* Better Demand Planning: Predictive analytics help Unilever adjust inventory levels, reducing overproduction.

* Greater Resilience: By simulating various scenarios, Unilever avoids costly supply chain failures.

By 2030, digital twins will be an essential tool for predictive maintenance, supply chain management, and process optimization, forming the foundation of the industrial metaverse.

3.3 Virtual Reality (VR) and Augmented Reality (AR) in Smart Factories

The Role of Immersive Technologies in Industry

* Virtual Reality (VR) creates fully simulated environments for industrial training, design, and process optimization.

* Augmented Reality (AR) overlays real-time digital information onto the physical world, helping workers visualize equipment performance and detect issues.

Current Challenges in Factory Operations

- Workforce Training Costs: Training employees on complex machinery is time-consuming and expensive.
- High Error Rates: Lack of real-time guidance leads to operational errors and inefficiencies.
- Remote Troubleshooting Difficulties: Fixing machine failures often requires on-site experts, increasing downtime.

Solution: VR & AR for Factory Operations

VR and AR technologies enhance efficiency by providing immersive, real-time data visualization tools.

How they work:

- VR Training Simulations – Employees learn in a risk-free environment without disrupting real production.
- AR for Maintenance & Troubleshooting – Smart glasses overlay digital instructions for workers to follow in real-time.
- Remote Collaboration – AR-powered remote assistance allows experts to guide workers from anywhere, reducing downtime.

Benefits of VR & AR in Smart Factories

* 30% Faster Repairs: Honeywell's AR-powered smart glasses reduce maintenance times significantly.

* 40% Error Reduction: Boeing's AR assembly system decreases wiring errors by 40%.

* Lower Training Costs: VR eliminates the need for physical training equipment, reducing expenses.

By 2030, VR and AR will significantly enhance industrial operations, reducing errors, improving efficiency, and increasing worker safety.

Applications of VR and AR in Industrial Automation

Remote Maintenance and Troubleshooting

* Honeywell's AR-powered smart glasses allow technicians to diagnose issues remotely, reducing repair times by 30%.

* Boeing uses AR for aircraft assembly, overlaying digital instructions on physical components, reducing wiring errors by 40%.

Current Challenges in Factory Operations

- Workforce Training Costs: Training employees on complex machinery is time-consuming and expensive.
- High Error Rates: Lack of real-time guidance leads to operational errors and inefficiencies.
- Remote Troubleshooting Difficulties: Fixing machine failures often requires on-site experts, increasing downtime.

Solution: VR & AR for Factory Operations

VR and AR technologies enhance efficiency by providing immersive, real-time data visualization tools.

How they work:

- VR Training Simulations – Employees learn in a risk-free environment without disrupting real production.
- AR for Maintenance & Troubleshooting – Smart glasses overlay digital instructions for workers to follow in real-time.
- Remote Collaboration – AR-powered remote assistance allows experts to guide workers from anywhere, reducing downtime.

Benefits of VR & AR in Smart Factories

* 30% Faster Repairs: Honeywell's AR-powered smart glasses reduce maintenance times significantly.

* 40% Error Reduction: Boeing's AR assembly system decreases wiring errors by 40%.

* Lower Training Costs: VR eliminates the need for physical training equipment, reducing expenses.

By 2030, VR and AR will be standard tools for industrial automation, revolutionizing training, maintenance, and real-time monitoring.

Workforce Training and Safety

* Oil & gas companies use AR simulations to train engineers on complex drilling operations without real-world risks.

Current Challenges in Oil & Gas Training

The oil and gas industry faces multiple challenges when training engineers and field operators, particularly for complex drilling operations:

1. High-Risk Work Environments
* Drilling operations occur in hazardous environments such as offshore rigs or high-pressure drilling sites.
* Mistakes in training can lead to safety incidents, environmental damage, or costly equipment failures.
1. Limited Hands-On Training Opportunities
* New engineers often struggle to gain practical experience due to the high costs and risks of real-world training.
* Physical drills and live training exercises are expensive and require shutdowns of operational equipment, impacting productivity.
1. Inconsistent Training Quality
* Traditional training relies on instructor-led programs, which can vary in effectiveness.

- A lack of standardized training methods leads to skill gaps among engineers, increasing the risk of operational errors.
1. Long Learning Curve and High Costs
- Mastering drilling operations requires years of experience, making it difficult to train employees quickly.
- Travel and on-site training costs are significant, especially for remote offshore locations.

Solution: AI-Powered AR Simulations for Drilling Training

To overcome these challenges, oil & gas companies are adopting AI-powered Augmented Reality (AR) simulations for training. These simulations provide a safe, cost-effective, and immersive learning experience for engineers.

Here's how AR simulations work:

1. Immersive Virtual Drilling Environments
- AR headsets overlay digital drilling scenarios onto the real-world workspace, allowing engineers to practice operations in a risk-free environment.
- AI-powered simulations mimic realistic drilling conditions, such as pressure fluctuations, mechanical failures, or hazardous gas leaks.
1. Interactive, Hands-On Learning
- Trainees can virtually operate drilling rigs, learning how to adjust drilling parameters, handle unexpected issues, and respond to emergencies.
- AR systems provide step-by-step interactive guidance, reducing reliance on classroom-based instruction.
1. AI-Driven Performance Analysis and Feedback
- AI tracks trainees' performance in real-time, identifying mistakes, slow response times, and areas for improvement.

- Engineers receive instant feedback, allowing them to refine their skills before working on live equipment.
1. Remote Training Capabilities
- AR-based training allows engineers to learn from any location, eliminating the need for costly travel to drilling sites.
- Senior experts can remotely oversee training sessions, ensuring consistency across global operations.

Benefits of AR-Based Drilling Training in the Oil & Gas Industry

* Improved Safety:

- AR eliminates the risks of real-world training accidents, making it safer for new engineers.
- Engineers learn to handle emergencies in a controlled, virtual environment before working on actual rigs.

* Cost Savings:

- Reduces the need for physical training equipment, on-site drills, and travel expenses.
- Companies save millions in operational costs by avoiding unnecessary rig downtime.

* Faster Skill Development:

- Engineers learn complex drilling procedures more quickly through hands-on, interactive training.
- AI-driven performance tracking helps accelerate learning curves.

* Standardized Training for Global Teams:

- AR ensures that all engineers receive consistent, high-quality training, regardless of their location.

- Companies can train large teams simultaneously, reducing onboarding time.

By 2030, AI-powered AR simulations will become the standard training method in oil & gas, ensuring faster, safer, and more cost-effective workforce development.

Real-Time Process Visualization

* AI-powered AR dashboards help factory workers monitor real-time machine performance, improving response times to failures.

Current Challenges in Industrial Machine Monitoring

Manufacturers face multiple challenges in monitoring machine performance and preventing equipment failures:

1. Delayed Response to Equipment Failures
- Traditional monitoring systems rely on manual inspections, leading to slow response times when issues arise.
- A lack of real-time visibility means that small malfunctions can go unnoticed until they escalate into major failures.
1. Complex Machinery with High Downtime Costs
- Modern factories use sophisticated machines that require constant monitoring to maintain peak performance.
- Unplanned equipment failures can halt production lines, causing millions in lost revenue.
1. Inefficient Data Access and Decision-Making
- Factory workers often rely on computer terminals or printed reports to check machine status.
- By the time issues are identified, production losses may have already occurred.
1. Skill Gaps Among Workers
- Many workers lack the technical expertise to diagnose machine failures quickly.

- Without real-time digital guidance, operators struggle to troubleshoot and fix issues efficiently.

Solution: AI-Powered AR Dashboards for Machine Monitoring

To address these challenges, manufacturers are implementing AI-driven AR dashboards that provide real-time, interactive machine performance data.

How it works:

1. Real-Time Sensor Data Visualization
- AR glasses or tablet-based dashboards overlay live performance metrics on physical machines.
- Operators can instantly see temperature, vibration, and operational efficiency without accessing separate screens.
1. AI-Powered Anomaly Detection
- AI continuously analyzes sensor data from factory machines to detect early warning signs of potential failures.
- The system alerts workers before critical breakdowns occur, preventing unplanned downtime.
1. Guided Troubleshooting with Augmented Reality
- If an issue is detected, AR displays step-by-step repair instructions directly on the machine.
- AI-powered assistants guide workers on which components to inspect or replace, reducing reliance on maintenance teams.
1. Remote Expert Assistance via AR
- If additional support is needed, remote engineers can see what the worker sees through AR and provide real-time guidance.
- This allows for faster problem resolution, even when senior technicians are not on-site.

Benefits of AI-Powered AR Dashboards in Manufacturing

* 30% Faster Response Times:

- Instant access to real-time machine data enables workers to address issues before they escalate.
- Reduces reliance on manual inspections that slow down problem detection.

* Reduced Downtime and Maintenance Costs:

- AI-driven anomaly detection prevents major equipment failures, saving manufacturers millions in lost productivity.
- AR-guided troubleshooting allows workers to resolve problems faster, minimizing downtime.

* Improved Worker Efficiency and Decision-Making:

- AR dashboards provide actionable insights at a glance, eliminating the need for manual data interpretation.
- Operators make faster, data-driven decisions, improving overall factory efficiency.

* Bridging the Skill Gap for New Workers:

- AI-powered AR systems act as virtual trainers, helping less-experienced workers quickly learn complex machine operations.
- Reduces the need for specialized on-site technical teams, making operations more scalable.

By 2030, AI-powered AR dashboards will be standard in smart factories, transforming industrial monitoring and maintenance into a proactive, highly efficient process.

AI as the Driving Force of the Industrial Metaverse

Artificial Intelligence (AI) is essential in enabling smart, self-optimizing factories within the industrial metaverse. AI-powered digital twins continuously learn from real-world data and suggest improvements, optimizing efficiency and reducing downtime.

Key AI Technologies Driving Process Optimization

* Machine Learning: AI analyzes historical production data to detect inefficiencies and suggest improvements.

* Computer Vision: AI-powered cameras monitor defects on production lines, reducing waste.

* Natural Language Processing (NLP): AI chatbots assist engineers in troubleshooting equipment failures.

Case Study: NVIDIA Omniverse & AI-Powered Digital Twins

NVIDIA's Omniverse platform allows companies to create highly detailed AI-driven digital twins. Companies like BMW use Omniverse to simulate entire production plants, optimizing processes before making real-world changes.

Current Challenges in Industrial Process Optimization

Despite the growing adoption of digital twins, industries face several challenges in effectively implementing and utilizing these advanced simulations:

High Complexity in Manufacturing and Supply Chains

- Modern production plants have thousands of interconnected processes, machines, and workers, making it difficult to understand dependencies and inefficiencies.

- Traditional static process models struggle to capture real-time operational complexities, leading to suboptimal decision-making.

Delayed Process Optimization Due to Real-World Testing

- Making physical changes to production lines is costly and time-consuming.
- Manufacturers often need to conduct trial-and-error experiments on live production systems, risking downtime, defects, and lost revenue.

Data Silos and Lack of Real-Time Insights

- Many companies store operational data in separate, unconnected systems, making it difficult to gain a holistic view of factory performance.
- Without real-time insights, manufacturers rely on historical data, making it hard to anticipate and adapt to changing conditions.

High Costs of Implementing Digital Twins

- Creating a highly detailed, real-time digital twin requires significant investment in computing power, AI models, and sensor networks.
- Many companies lack the necessary infrastructure to support large-scale, AI-driven digital twin simulations.

Solution: NVIDIA Omniverse for AI-Powered Digital Twins

NVIDIA's Omniverse provides a powerful real-time simulation and collaboration platform, integrating AI, IoT, and 3D visualization to create highly realistic, AI-driven digital twins.

How Omniverse Solves Key Industry Challenges:

AI-Driven Simulation of Complex Manufacturing Environments

- Omniverse creates a fully interactive 3D replica of production plants, integrating real-world data in real time.
- AI algorithms simulate production processes, identify inefficiencies, and predict potential failures before they happen.
- Engineers can test new production layouts, machine configurations, and process improvements without disrupting operations.

* Example: BMW uses Omniverse digital twins to simulate entire factory operations, optimizing worker movement, robotic workflows, and machine interactions, reducing inefficiencies by 30%.

Real-Time Process Optimization with AI

- Omniverse continuously analyzes production data, adjusting models dynamically based on live sensor feedback.
- AI simulations predict how changes in one part of the process will impact the entire system, enabling data-driven decision-making.
- Manufacturers can test and refine optimizations virtually before implementing them physically, reducing trial-and-error costs.

* Example: BMW uses Omniverse simulations to fine-tune factory layouts, reducing worker movement inefficiencies by 15% and increasing automation accuracy.

Breaking Down Data Silos with a Unified Industrial Metaverse

- Omniverse connects different data sources, including IoT devices, CAD models, AI analytics, and enterprise software.
- Manufacturers can visualize and analyze every aspect of production in a single, unified 3D environment.

- AI processes vast amounts of real-time data, providing instant insights and automated optimization suggestions.

* Example: Instead of manually checking for defects, AI-powered Omniverse simulations detect anomalies in BMW's production process in real-time, improving quality control by 25%.

Cost-Effective Deployment with Cloud and Edge Computing

- Omniverse leverages cloud and edge computing, allowing companies to run large-scale AI-driven digital twins without requiring massive on-site infrastructure investments.
- Manufacturers can access simulations from anywhere, enabling global teams to collaborate in real time.
- AI-driven digital twins reduce reliance on costly trial runs and physical prototyping, lowering operational costs over time.

* Example: Omniverse allowed BMW to simulate the integration of 31 factories worldwide, reducing coordination errors and ensuring global production efficiency.

Benefits of NVIDIA Omniverse in Industrial Automation

By integrating AI, real-time data, and digital twins, NVIDIA Omniverse delivers significant advantages for manufacturers and industrial automation leaders.

Faster and More Efficient Process Optimization

* AI-powered simulations allow companies to test process changes virtually before implementing them, reducing optimization cycles by 40%.

* Reduces the need for physical prototypes, cutting down on waste and production disruptions.

Lower Operational Costs and Increased Profitability

* Predictive maintenance simulations reduce unplanned downtime, improving equipment efficiency and extending machine lifespan.

* AI-driven optimizations result in higher production output with fewer resources, improving profit margins.

Improved Quality Control and Defect Reduction

* AI detects anomalies and inefficiencies in real-time, allowing companies to address defects before they impact production.

* Reduces the number of defective products, improving customer satisfaction and reducing rework costs.

Enhanced Workforce Collaboration and Training

* Global teams can collaborate in shared virtual environments, testing new ideas without travel or physical prototyping.

* Digital twins provide immersive training experiences, helping engineers and operators learn in a risk-free environment.

Sustainability and Energy Efficiency

* AI optimizes energy usage, reducing factory carbon footprints by up to 20%.

* Companies can simulate green energy integration, ensuring a smoother transition to renewable power sources.

By 2030, AI-driven process optimization will enable factories to be autonomous, efficient, and adaptive, revolutionizing industrial automation.

3.5 Human-Machine Collaboration in the Industrial Metaverse

The Future of Human-AI Interaction

The industrial metaverse will not replace human workers—but enhance them. AI, robotics, and immersive technologies will allow seamless collaboration between human workers and machines.

How the Industrial Metaverse Enhances Workforce Collaboration

* AI-Powered Virtual Assistants: Engineers receive real-time AI recommendations to improve efficiency.

* Digital Co-Working Spaces: VR-powered environments allow remote teams to collaborate in real time.

* AR-Assisted Manufacturing: AR provides workers with real-time instructions, improving accuracy and reducing errors.

Case Study: Ford's Use of VR for Collaborative Design

Virtual Reality (VR) is transforming the way automotive manufacturers like Ford design, test, and refine vehicle prototypes. By leveraging VR, Ford enables its global design teams to collaborate in real-time, eliminating the need for costly physical prototypes and accelerating product development. The use of VR in automotive design significantly reduces development costs, enhances design accuracy, and speeds up time-to-market.

However, before Ford integrated VR into its workflow, the company faced several challenges that are common in traditional vehicle design. The introduction of VR-powered collaborative design platforms has provided innovative solutions that deliver significant benefits to the automotive industry.

Current Challenges in Traditional Vehicle Design

Despite advancements in computer-aided design (CAD) and simulation software, the automotive industry still encounters major hurdles in vehicle design and prototyping.

Lengthy and Costly Design Iterations

- Designing a new vehicle model requires multiple prototype versions, often leading to extensive revisions before production begins.
- Each physical prototype can cost millions of dollars and take weeks or months to build.
- Design iterations rely on in-person collaboration, which slows down the process, especially with globally distributed teams.

Inefficient Cross-Team Collaboration

- Ford has design teams, engineers, and stakeholders located worldwide. Traditional design reviews required expensive travel, making real-time collaboration difficult.
- Design teams often worked in silos, leading to misalignment and costly rework later in the development cycle.
- Evaluating ergonomics, usability, and assembly feasibility was difficult without a real-world prototype, leading to design flaws being detected late in the process.

Physical Space and Resource Constraints

- Developing physical prototypes requires large-scale facilities equipped with expensive tools and resources.
- Limited access to prototype vehicles made it challenging for all team members to fully visualize and interact with the design.
- Making even minor adjustments required significant time and material investments, further delaying production schedules.

Risk of Late Design Errors

- Without interactive real-time feedback, many design flaws were only discovered after a prototype was built, requiring costly modifications.
- Ergonomic testing, crash simulations, and aesthetic refinements often needed multiple physical test cycles, increasing production delays.
- Engineers had limited ways to test assembly feasibility before manufacturing, leading to unexpected manufacturing bottlenecks.

Solution: Ford's Use of VR for Collaborative Vehicle Design

To address these challenges, Ford implemented a Virtual Reality (VR)-based collaborative design platform, allowing global teams to work together in a shared virtual space.

How Ford's VR Solution Works:

Real-Time VR Collaboration for Global Teams

- Ford's VR platform enables designers, engineers, and decision-makers from different locations to enter a shared virtual workspace.
- Using VR headsets, teams visualize, modify, and interact with full-scale 3D vehicle models in real time.
- Stakeholders from manufacturing, safety, and marketing departments can provide instant feedback without needing a physical prototype.

* Example: Ford's design teams in the U.S., Europe, and China can simultaneously evaluate a car model in VR, reducing design alignment meetings by 40%.

Rapid Prototyping with Virtual Models

- Instead of building multiple physical prototypes, Ford now creates interactive VR vehicle models, allowing for instant design modifications.
- Engineers can test aerodynamics, crash performance, and material properties within the VR environment, reducing the need for costly physical tests.
- AI-powered simulations allow Ford to test multiple design variations simultaneously without wasting materials.

* Example: A small design tweak, such as adjusting the dashboard layout, can be tested and approved in VR within hours instead of weeks.

Ergonomic and Safety Testing in Virtual Environments

- Ford's VR system allows designers to evaluate ergonomics and driver interaction before producing a physical model.
- Engineers can simulate different driving conditions, ensuring optimal visibility, comfort, and control placement.
- VR crash simulations help detect potential safety issues early, improving overall vehicle design.

* Example: Ford used VR to redesign seat placement and dashboard reachability, reducing driver strain and improving accessibility.

VR for Assembly Line Planning and Manufacturing Feasibility

- Ford's manufacturing teams use VR to simulate the vehicle assembly process, identifying potential production bottlenecks before manufacturing begins.
- Workers can practice assembling vehicle components in VR, ensuring that designs are optimized for real-world manufacturing.
- VR-based training improves worker efficiency, reducing errors in final assembly.

* Example: Ford detected an assembly misalignment issue in VR, preventing a $500,000 tooling adjustment before production started.

Benefits of VR-Based Collaborative Design in Automotive Manufacturing

By integrating VR into vehicle design and prototyping, Ford has achieved significant cost savings, efficiency improvements, and faster product development cycles.

Faster Design Iterations and Shorter Development Time

* VR reduces design iteration cycles from months to weeks, allowing Ford to launch new models faster.

* Design teams can quickly refine concepts, improving innovation and creativity.

* Ford estimates that VR collaboration has cut development time by 25%, allowing for faster time-to-market.

Reduced Costs Through Virtual Prototyping

* Eliminating the need for multiple physical prototypes has saved Ford millions of dollars annually.

* AI-driven simulations reduce the need for expensive wind tunnel tests and crash tests.

* Material waste is significantly reduced, contributing to Ford's sustainability goals.

Enhanced Global Collaboration and Real-Time Feedback

* Ford's global teams can collaborate in VR without travel, reducing meeting-related expenses and delays.

* Instant feedback from design, engineering, and manufacturing teams improves overall product quality.

* Decisions that used to take weeks can now be made in real time, accelerating production timelines.

Improved Vehicle Ergonomics and Safety

* Designers can evaluate seat positioning, dashboard layouts, and visibility before building a physical model.

* VR crash testing allows for safer vehicle designs without using expensive test vehicles.

* Ford has improved ergonomic comfort and driver accessibility, increasing customer satisfaction.

Smarter and More Efficient Manufacturing Planning

* VR helps Ford detect assembly inefficiencies early, ensuring a smoother manufacturing process.

* Worker training in VR has reduced onboarding times, improving production efficiency.

* Fewer last-minute design changes reduce disruptions in the manufacturing pipeline.

Conclusion: The Future of VR in Automotive Design

By 2030, VR-based collaborative design will become an industry standard in automotive and industrial manufacturing. Companies like Ford have demonstrated that VR enhances design efficiency, lowers costs, and speeds up production, paving the way for a new era of digital prototyping.

As VR technology continues to advance, manufacturers will integrate AI-powered design assistants, real-time physics simulations, and fully immersive collaboration spaces, further optimizing product development.

By 2030, the industrial workforce will rely on AI-driven collaboration tools, improving productivity and job satisfaction.

3.6 The Future of the Industrial Metaverse (2030 and Beyond)

How the Industrial Metaverse Will Evolve

By 2030, industries will operate in fully digitalized environments where AI, digital twins, and immersive technologies enable seamless automation.

Key future developments include:

* Hyper-realistic Digital Twins powered by AI and quantum computing.

* Metaverse-Based Industrial Marketplaces where companies buy and sell digital models of machinery and production lines.

* AI-Powered Predictive Analytics capable of self-healing industrial systems.

Key Challenges and Considerations

* Cybersecurity Risks: The industrial metaverse will require robust security to prevent cyber threats.

* Data Privacy Concerns: AI-powered systems will need transparent and ethical data policies.

* Workforce Reskilling: Employees must be trained in AI, VR, and metaverse technologies to remain competitive.

By 2030, the industrial metaverse—powered by digital twins, AI, VR, and AR—will transform industrial automation. Companies that embrace these technologies will:

* Optimize operations and reduce costs

* Improve workforce collaboration and training

* Enhance sustainability through AI-driven energy optimization

Final Thoughts

The industrial metaverse is not just a trend—it's the future of manufacturing, logistics, and energy. Businesses that invest in digital transformation today will lead the next industrial revolution by 2030 and beyond.

Key Takeaways:

✔ Digital Twins will be standard for predictive maintenance & process optimization.

✔ VR and AR will enhance workforce training, remote monitoring & maintenance.

✔ AI-powered process optimization will make factories self-optimizing & autonomous.

✔ Human-machine collaboration will improve productivity & workplace safety.

By 2030, the industrial metaverse will be a reality—driving the next wave of efficiency, innovation, and sustainability in industrial automation.

Trend #3 - Sustainable and Energy-Efficient Automation

4.0 Introduction

Sustainability is no longer a choice—it is a necessity. As industries strive to reduce their carbon footprint and transition toward **energy-efficient automation**, they face growing pressure from **governments, consumers, and investors**. By 2030, **sustainable automation** will become a defining characteristic of competitive businesses.

Industrial automation, historically associated with high energy consumption and material waste, is undergoing a **major transformation** toward **green and energy-efficient practices**. Companies are **integrating renewable energy sources**, implementing **circular economy models**, and leveraging **AI-driven energy optimization** to create smarter, more sustainable factories.

This chapter explores how industrial automation is evolving to support **carbon-neutral manufacturing, waste reduction, smart energy grids, and ESG compliance**, ensuring that industries not only remain competitive but also align with global sustainability goals.

4.1 Carbon-Neutral Manufacturing and Green Energy Integration

Current Challenges in Industrial Energy Consumption

Manufacturing and industrial processes account for nearly **30% of global energy consumption and 20% of CO_2 emissions**. The traditional energy sources used in factories, such as coal and natural gas, contribute significantly to environmental degradation. Industries face several **key challenges** in their journey toward carbon neutrality:

High Dependence on Fossil Fuels

- Many factories still rely on **coal, diesel, and natural gas**, making it difficult to transition to sustainable energy.
- Upgrading infrastructure for **renewable energy integration** requires substantial investment.

Energy Inefficiency in Production

- **Old machinery and inefficient processes** lead to high energy waste.
- Lack of **real-time monitoring** prevents companies from identifying energy optimization opportunities.

Fluctuations in Renewable Energy Supply

- Solar and wind power are **intermittent energy sources**, requiring industries to integrate **smart grids and energy storage systems**.
- Without proper **energy management strategies**, factories cannot fully utilize renewable energy sources.

Solution: Integrating Renewable Energy and Smart Energy Systems

Industries are adopting **carbon-neutral manufacturing strategies** by integrating **green energy solutions** such as:

On-Site Renewable Energy Generation

- **Factories are installing solar panels, wind turbines, and biomass energy systems** to generate power locally.

- Example: **Tesla's Gigafactory** in Nevada runs on 100% renewable energy, utilizing **solar, wind, and battery storage systems**.

AI-Driven Energy Optimization

- AI-powered energy management systems analyze **real-time energy consumption data** to identify inefficiencies.
- Smart **energy demand forecasting** allows industries to balance **renewable energy supply and demand**.

Energy Storage and Grid Integration

- Factories integrate **battery storage systems** to store excess solar and wind energy for **continuous production**.
- Smart grids enable factories to **sell surplus energy back to the power grid**, improving sustainability and profitability.

Benefits of Carbon-Neutral Manufacturing

* **Lower Operational Costs** – Companies that switch to renewable energy experience **long-term cost reductions** by reducing reliance on fossil fuels.

* **Reduced Carbon Footprint** – Transitioning to **clean energy sources** helps companies meet **net-zero emission targets**.

* **Regulatory Compliance** – Many governments offer **tax incentives** and grants for industries adopting green energy solutions.

Current Challenges in Industrial Waste Management

Traditional manufacturing follows a **linear economy model: extract, manufacture, use, and dispose**. This leads to excessive waste, pollution, and resource depletion. Industries face the following key waste management challenges:

Overproduction and Excessive Material Waste

- Many production lines **generate large amounts of scrap materials** that cannot be recycled or reused.

Lack of Efficient Recycling Systems

- Industries struggle with **recycling complex materials** such as electronic waste, composite materials, and hazardous chemicals.

High Costs of Waste Disposal

- Companies **spend billions on waste management**, increasing **operational costs** and **environmental impact**.

Solution: Implementing Circular Economy Models

A **circular economy** focuses on designing products and processes that **minimize waste, maximize resource efficiency, and promote recycling**. Key strategies include:

Industrial Symbiosis and Material Reuse

- Factories create **closed-loop systems** where waste from one process becomes a raw material for another.

- Example: **Renault's circular economy initiative** recycles **95% of materials** in end-of-life vehicles.

AI-Powered Smart Waste Management

- AI systems monitor and classify **industrial waste in real-time**, helping industries separate **recyclable materials from waste**.
- **Automated robotic sorting** increases recycling efficiency, reducing landfill waste.

3D Printing and Sustainable Manufacturing

- 3D printing enables **on-demand production**, reducing material waste.
- Companies use **recycled plastic and metal powders** to manufacture new parts.

Benefits of Circular Economy in Industrial Automation

* **Waste Reduction** – A **zero-waste** approach lowers production costs and minimizes environmental damage.

* **Improved Supply Chain Sustainability** – Reusing materials decreases dependence on raw material extraction.

* **Regulatory Advantages** – Governments offer **carbon credits and incentives** for industries implementing circular economy models.

4.3 AI-Driven Energy Optimization and Smart Grids in Factories

Current Challenges in Industrial Energy Efficiency

Industrial automation systems are often **energy-intensive**, consuming vast amounts of electricity for production, lighting, heating, and cooling. The major challenges include:

Unoptimized Energy Usage

- **Factories lack real-time energy monitoring**, leading to **excessive power consumption** in non-essential operations.

Inconsistent Energy Demand and Load Management

- **Peak energy usage spikes** increase electricity costs, affecting profitability.

Lack of Predictive Maintenance for Energy Efficiency

- Energy waste occurs due to **unnoticed leaks, malfunctioning equipment, and poor maintenance**.

Solution: AI-Driven Energy Optimization & Smart Grids

AI-powered energy management systems use **machine learning algorithms** to:

Monitor and Optimize Energy Usage

- AI sensors **analyze power consumption patterns** and suggest **energy-efficient scheduling**.
- Example: **Google's AI-driven cooling system** for data centers reduced energy usage by **40%**.

Predictive Maintenance for Energy Efficiency

- AI detects **inefficiencies in machinery**, preventing unnecessary power wastage.
- Smart factories automate **equipment shutdowns during low-demand periods**.

Integration of Smart Grids and Demand Response Systems

- **Factories integrate smart grids** to optimize electricity usage based on **real-time energy prices**.
- AI systems **predict energy demand** and shift production schedules accordingly.

Benefits of AI-Driven Energy Optimization

* **Lower Energy Bills** – AI reduces **energy waste**, improving cost savings.

* **Sustainable Production** – Smart energy grids help industries **reduce carbon emissions**.

* **Better Grid Resilience** – Factories **balance power demand**, avoiding blackouts and inefficiencies.

4.4 ESG Regulations and Their Impact on Industrial Automation

Current Challenges in Meeting ESG Compliance

Environmental, Social, and Governance (**ESG**) regulations are reshaping industrial automation, pushing companies to **adopt greener technologies**. However, industries struggle with:

Complex Regulatory Requirements

- Different countries enforce **varying ESG standards**, making compliance challenging.

High Costs of ESG Compliance

- Implementing **eco-friendly technologies** requires **capital investment**, discouraging some companies.

Data Transparency & Reporting

- Factories must **track and report energy usage, emissions, and sustainability initiatives**, increasing administrative work.

Solution: ESG Compliance Through Automation & AI

Automated ESG Data Collection & Reporting

- AI-powered **data analytics platforms** track carbon emissions, energy consumption, and sustainability performance.

Investment in Sustainable Technologies

- Companies invest in **low-emission equipment, renewable energy, and smart automation** to meet regulatory standards.

Benefits of ESG Compliance in Industrial Automation

* **Access to Green Investments** – ESG-compliant companies attract **sustainability-focused investors**.

* **Regulatory Compliance & Avoiding Fines** – Automated ESG tracking ensures factories **meet legal requirements**.

* **Improved Brand Reputation** – Sustainable manufacturing enhances **customer and stakeholder trust**.

Case Study 1: Tesla's Gigafactories – Achieving Carbon-Neutral Manufacturing

Current Challenges

High Energy Demand

- Tesla's Gigafactories require **massive amounts of energy** to produce electric vehicle (EV) batteries, which initially relied on traditional power grids.
- Transitioning to a **fully renewable energy model** was complex due to fluctuations in solar and wind energy availability.

Raw Material Sourcing & Waste Generation

- Battery production involves materials like **lithium, cobalt, and nickel**, raising concerns over mining sustainability and waste disposal.

Supply Chain Carbon Footprint

- Manufacturing and transporting battery components contribute to **indirect emissions** beyond factory operations.

Solution: Transition to 100% Renewable Energy

On-Site Renewable Energy Integration

- Tesla built **solar farms** and **energy storage systems** at its Gigafactories, allowing operations to run entirely on **solar and wind energy**.

Battery Recycling and Circular Economy

- Tesla developed **closed-loop recycling** for battery materials, reducing the demand for new raw materials and lowering emissions.

Smart Grid & AI-Powered Energy Management

- AI-based systems **forecast energy demand** and optimize **battery storage and usage**, ensuring energy reliability.

Benefits

* **Carbon-Neutral Manufacturing** – Tesla's Gigafactory in Nevada operates on **100% renewable energy**, reducing CO_2 emissions by millions of tons annually.

* **Lower Energy Costs** – On-site solar panels and battery storage lower **operational electricity expenses**.

* **Supply Chain Sustainability – Recycling and reusing battery materials** reduce dependency on new mining operations.

Case Study 2: Unilever's Circular Economy and Smart Waste Management

Current Challenges

Excessive Packaging Waste

- Unilever produces millions of consumer products, leading to **large-scale plastic and packaging waste**.

Difficulties in Recycling & Waste Sorting

- Many packaging materials were **not easily recyclable**, causing landfill accumulation.

High Cost of Sustainable Alternatives

- Transitioning to biodegradable materials required significant **R&D investment** and **logistical changes**.

Solution: Implementing Circular Economy & Smart Waste Management

AI-Powered Waste Sorting & Recycling

- Unilever deployed **AI-driven waste sorting machines** to separate recyclable plastics more efficiently.

Reusable and Compostable Packaging

- The company introduced **refillable bottles and compostable materials**, reducing single-use plastic waste.

Collaboration with Supply Chain Partners

- Unilever worked with suppliers to develop **low-carbon footprint materials** and improved recycling infrastructure.

Benefits

* **Waste Reduction** – By **eliminating over 100,000 tons of plastic waste**, Unilever is closer to its zero-waste goals.

* **Lower Carbon Footprint** – Sustainable materials reduce **manufacturing-related CO_2 emissions**.

* **Cost Savings & Consumer Appeal** – Customers prefer eco-friendly products, increasing **brand loyalty** and sales.

Case Study 3: Google's AI-Driven Energy Optimization for Data Centers

Current Challenges

High Energy Consumption in Data Centers

- Google's data centers require **massive cooling systems**, consuming large amounts of electricity.

Inefficient Cooling Strategies

- Traditional cooling systems led to **unnecessary energy waste**, increasing operational costs.

Peak Energy Demand & Grid Load

- Energy demand spikes created **grid instability**, increasing costs during peak hours.

Solution: AI-Powered Smart Energy Optimization

DeepMind AI for Predictive Cooling

- Google used **AI algorithms** from DeepMind to optimize cooling by predicting temperature fluctuations.

Smart Grid Integration & Renewable Energy Use

- The company adopted **smart grids**, allowing seamless transitions between **solar, wind, and grid power**.

Automated Demand Response

- AI adjusted data center workloads to operate at **low-energy periods**, reducing **peak electricity demand**.

Benefits

* **40% Reduction in Cooling Energy Usage** – AI-driven optimization significantly lowered operational energy consumption.

* **Lower Carbon Footprint** – Transitioning to **100% renewable energy** reduced emissions.

* **Cost Savings & Scalability** – AI automation allows **smoother global expansion** of Google's data centers.

Case Study 4: Siemens Smart Grid Integration for Sustainable Factories

Current Challenges

Fluctuating Renewable Energy Availability

- Factories need **consistent power**, but renewables like **solar and wind** are intermittent.

High Industrial Energy Costs

- Energy expenses account for a significant portion of **manufacturing costs**, impacting profitability.

Lack of Real-Time Energy Optimization

- Traditional factories lack **smart monitoring systems** to efficiently balance **energy supply and demand**.

Solution: AI-Enabled Smart Grids & Energy Management

Smart Grid Integration

- Siemens connected factories to **smart grids**, allowing them to **automatically adjust energy usage** based on real-time grid conditions.

Battery Storage for Renewable Energy

- **Energy storage systems** help factories use stored solar/wind power during low production periods.

AI-Based Load Balancing & Predictive Energy Demand

- Siemens' AI analyzes energy usage **patterns**, adjusting machine operations **to avoid peak-hour consumption**.

Benefits

* **20% Reduction in Energy Costs** – Factories operate on the **most cost-effective energy sources**.

* **Increased Energy Efficiency** – AI-driven systems minimize **energy waste** and improve sustainability.

* **Better Resilience & Power Stability** – Smart grids prevent **power outages and overloading**.

Case Study 5: Schneider Electric's ESG Automation for Industrial Compliance

Current Challenges

Strict Global ESG Regulations

- Many industries struggle to comply with evolving **sustainability laws and carbon reporting requirements**.

Manual ESG Data Collection & Reporting

- Traditional ESG tracking methods involve **complex paperwork and human error**, making compliance difficult.

High Initial Investment in Green Technologies

- Implementing **low-carbon automation** requires significant upfront investment.

Solution: AI-Driven ESG Compliance & Automation

Automated ESG Reporting Systems

- Schneider Electric developed **AI-based software** to collect **real-time carbon emissions and energy usage data**.

Smart Building & Factory Automation

- AI optimizes **HVAC, lighting, and production lines** to reduce emissions and **increase efficiency**.

Blockchain for Transparent ESG Data

- The company uses **blockchain** to create **tamper-proof records** of sustainability metrics.

Benefits

* **Easier ESG Compliance** – AI automates sustainability reporting, **reducing administrative workload**.

* **Higher Investor Confidence** – Transparent data improves **investment opportunities** for green businesses.

* **Energy & Cost Savings** – Smart automation reduces **electricity consumption** and **carbon taxes**.

Conclusion: The Future of Sustainable Automation

By 2030, industries will adopt **AI-powered energy optimization, smart grids, circular economy models, and ESG compliance strategies** to drive sustainable automation. The shift toward **green manufacturing** will not only benefit the environment but also create **long-term profitability and efficiency**.

Trend #4: Hyperconnected Industrial Ecosystems (5G & IIoT)

The future of industrial automation is **hyperconnected, intelligent, and real-time**. The emergence of **5G, Edge Computing, AI-driven Industrial Internet of Things (IIoT), Blockchain, and Cyber-Physical Systems (CPS)** is revolutionizing manufacturing by **seamlessly connecting machines, devices, and systems**. These technologies are eliminating delays, optimizing efficiency, and making factories more autonomous than ever before.

By **2030**, hyperconnected industrial ecosystems will become the **foundation of Industry 4.0 and Industry 5.0**, enabling seamless collaboration across global manufacturing networks.

5.1 The Role of 5G and Ultra-Reliable Low-Latency Communication (URLLC)

The role of **5G** in industrial automation is transforming how factories communicate and operate. Traditional manufacturing environments have relied heavily on wired networks or older wireless technologies like Wi-Fi and 4G to support their industrial processes. However, these systems often face significant limitations when it comes to handling the enormous amount of data produced by connected devices. **5G technology** brings a leap forward in terms of speed, latency, and reliability, making it an ideal solution for modern industrial ecosystems.

One of the major challenges faced by industries in implementing automation has been **network latency**. Industrial robots, sensors, and automated systems require precise, real-time data transmission to make split-second decisions. Older networks like 4G, Wi-Fi, and Ethernet suffer from high latency, leading to delays in the execution of tasks, which in turn affects the overall efficiency and productivity of the factory. For example, a delay of even a few milliseconds in transmitting data could result in production errors, defects in manufactured products, or the failure of a critical machine part.

5G and Ultra-Reliable Low-Latency Communication (URLLC) tackle these challenges by offering **data transfer speeds** up to **100 times faster than 4G**, with latency reduced to as low as **1 millisecond**. This significant reduction in latency makes it possible for industrial systems to communicate instantaneously, enabling real-time machine control and automated decision-making. Whether it is coordinating robotic arms, controlling automated guided vehicles (AGVs), or managing complex manufacturing processes, the **5G-enabled industrial network** ensures that all devices work together smoothly and efficiently.

Additionally, the shift from wired connections to **wireless networks** powered by **5G** brings immense flexibility and scalability to factories. In traditional setups, manufacturing units are often confined to a network of **wired connections**, requiring substantial investments in infrastructure and maintenance. 5G allows for the creation of flexible, wireless networks that can scale with the growing number of connected devices on the factory floor. This significantly reduces the cost and complexity of network infrastructure, providing manufacturers with the ability to expand and adapt their operations without the need for extensive rewiring or new hardware.

Security is another crucial factor in industrial automation. Traditional communication networks are often susceptible to cyberattacks, which can jeopardize sensitive data, disrupt operations, and cause costly downtime. With 5G, manufacturers can deploy **private industrial networks** with **network slicing**, providing dedicated, secure communication channels for different devices or applications. This approach ensures that critical systems are isolated from less-sensitive network traffic, enhancing the security of industrial operations and protecting data from unauthorized access.

In conclusion, **5G and URLLC** enable real-time automation, high-speed data transfer, and scalable wireless infrastructure, all while enhancing security and reliability. These features collectively ensure that industrial ecosystems can achieve higher levels of automation, reduce downtime, and improve productivity across the board.

5.2 Edge Computing and AI-Enabled Industrial Internet of Things (IIoT)

The rapid growth of the **Industrial Internet of Things (IIoT)** has led to an explosion in the volume of data generated by industrial machines, sensors, and devices. While cloud computing has traditionally been used to process and analyze this data, the inherent latency of cloud-based systems has become a bottleneck in industries that require real-time decision-making. As factories deploy more connected devices and sensors, the need for faster processing and analysis of data has given rise to **edge computing** as an effective solution.

Edge computing refers to the practice of processing data **locally** on devices or edge nodes, rather than sending it to a central cloud server. This significantly reduces the delay in data transmission, allowing industrial systems to make real-time decisions based on the data collected by machines and sensors. For example, in manufacturing plants where **predictive maintenance** is crucial, machines equipped with sensors can analyze their own performance in real-time and trigger maintenance actions before a failure occurs. This proactive approach not only reduces downtime but also improves equipment efficiency and lifespan.

One of the main advantages of edge computing is the **reduction of latency**. Cloud-based systems introduce delays as data has to be transferred over long distances to a central server for processing. By shifting the data processing to the **edge**, near the devices generating the data, industrial systems can operate in near real-time. This is especially important in industries like **automotive manufacturing, oil and gas**, and **food processing**, where millisecond-level delays in response time can lead to errors, equipment malfunctions, or costly mistakes.

Another key benefit of **edge computing** is **cost efficiency**. Data generated by industrial machines can be vast, with factories generating terabytes of information every day. Sending all of this data to the cloud for processing incurs significant costs related to **data storage** and **bandwidth usage**. By processing data locally at the edge, factories can minimize the amount of data transmitted to the cloud, reducing both **cloud storage costs** and **network bandwidth** requirements. This allows businesses to achieve higher operational efficiency while maintaining lower operational costs.

The integration of **AI** with edge computing enhances the capabilities of **IIoT systems**. With AI algorithms running directly on edge devices, real-time data can be processed and analyzed to provide insights on machine performance, predictive maintenance, and even quality control. AI models can learn from the data generated by sensors and equipment, allowing them to **predict failures** and recommend corrective actions without human intervention. This decentralized approach to data processing and decision-making ensures that factories remain operational, even in remote or disconnected environments.

In industries where network connectivity is limited or intermittent, such as **offshore oil rigs** or **mining operations**, edge computing ensures that **IIoT systems** continue to operate without disruption. Even if the connection to the central cloud is lost, edge devices can still process data and perform critical functions. Once the connection is restored, the data can be synced with the cloud, ensuring that the factory operations remain uninterrupted.

Ultimately, **edge computing and AI-enabled IIoT** systems enable faster decision-making, lower operational costs, and greater resilience in industrial environments. By bringing computational power closer to the devices, industries can achieve enhanced performance and reliability across their manufacturing processes.

5.3 Blockchain for Secure, Transparent Industrial Data Exchange

Blockchain technology has been gaining traction across various industries for its ability to provide **secure, transparent, and tamper-proof** data management. In industrial ecosystems, where multiple stakeholders are involved in the production, supply, and distribution of goods, blockchain offers a way to ensure **data integrity** and **accountability** at every stage of the process.

A major challenge in industrial operations is the **lack of transparency** and **trust** in data exchanges. Industrial supply chains often involve numerous parties, from raw material suppliers to manufacturers to distributors. In many cases, these entities rely on manual systems or outdated digital technologies to record and verify transactions, which can be prone to errors, fraud, and delays. This lack of transparency makes it difficult to ensure the authenticity of data and trace the origins of materials and components used in production.

Blockchain addresses these issues by creating an **immutable ledger** of all transactions that take place within a supply chain or industrial system. Each piece of data recorded on the blockchain is **encrypted** and **linked** to the previous data, creating a chain of information that cannot be tampered with or altered. This provides a **secure** and **verifiable record** of every transaction, from raw material sourcing to final product delivery. By using blockchain, manufacturers can ensure that their data is **secure**, reducing the risk of **cyberattacks** and **data breaches** that could disrupt operations.

Another benefit of blockchain in industrial environments is the use of **smart contracts**. These self-executing contracts automate the process of verifying and enforcing agreements between different parties. For example, a smart contract could automatically release payments once materials are delivered to a manufacturing plant or trigger the next step in the production process once specific quality standards are met. This reduces the potential for fraud, delays, and disputes, while ensuring that all parties fulfill their contractual obligations.

Additionally, blockchain provides **end-to-end traceability** for every component or material used in production. Whether it's tracking the source of raw materials, verifying the compliance of suppliers with regulatory standards, or ensuring the quality of finished products, blockchain enables complete transparency across the entire supply chain. This is particularly valuable in industries with stringent regulatory requirements, such as **pharmaceuticals**, **food production**, and **electronics manufacturing**, where compliance with safety and quality standards is critical.

In conclusion, blockchain technology enhances industrial data exchange by providing a **secure, transparent, and auditable** system for tracking transactions and verifying supply chain data. The use of **smart contracts** further automates industrial processes, reducing the risk of fraud, increasing operational efficiency, and ensuring compliance with industry standards.

5.4 Cyber-Physical Systems and Seamless Factory Connectivity

Cyber-Physical Systems (CPS) are an integral part of the **smart factory** ecosystem, where digital and physical systems interact seamlessly to enable real-time monitoring, automation, and control. CPSs combine physical machinery, sensors, and robots with digital technologies like **IoT**, **edge computing**, and **AI** to create a fully integrated and interconnected manufacturing environment.

A major challenge in traditional manufacturing setups is the **lack of integration** between digital and physical systems. Many factories still rely on **legacy machines** that are not connected to modern digital systems. As a result, these systems operate in silos, making it difficult to collect real-time data and coordinate operations. The absence of **interoperability** between different devices and systems can lead to inefficiencies, poor decision-making, and high operational costs.

CPS solves this problem by synchronizing the digital and physical components of a factory, creating a **unified system** that can monitor, control, and optimize operations in real-time. **Digital twins**, for example, are virtual replicas of physical systems that allow factory managers to simulate and analyze processes before making adjustments to the actual equipment. These real-time digital simulations provide critical insights into **machine health**, **production rates**, and **potential failures**, allowing operators to make data-driven decisions and prevent unexpected downtimes.

The implementation of CPS also requires standardization to ensure **interoperability** across different platforms and technologies. Using **open-source industrial protocols** and **industry standards**, CPS ensures that various machines, devices, and software platforms can communicate and work together seamlessly. This enables a more flexible and scalable manufacturing environment, where new devices and systems can be easily integrated into existing workflows without the need for extensive modifications.

By integrating **CPS** into manufacturing processes, industries can achieve **zero unplanned downtime**, **optimized efficiency**, and **seamless machine interoperability**. This allows factories to operate at peak productivity, with minimal human intervention, and respond dynamically to changes in demand, market conditions, or production requirements.

Case Study 1: Ericsson's 5G Smart Factory

Current Challenges

In the traditional manufacturing setup, communication between machines, robots, and systems in a factory was often constrained by slow network speeds, causing delays in data transmission. In Ericsson's previous factory models, manufacturing processes were heavily dependent on legacy systems that used **Wi-Fi or wired networks**. These networks had high latency, which affected the speed at which real-time data could be transferred between machines and control systems. As the demand for faster and more reliable automation grew, these networks struggled to keep up with the volume of data generated by the factory's equipment, especially for processes requiring real-time decisions.

Some of the primary challenges Ericsson faced before implementing 5G technology were:

- **Latency Issues:** A delay of even milliseconds could result in inefficient machine operation, errors in product quality, and increased downtime.
- **Network Congestion:** With the increasing number of devices and machines becoming connected, the factory network was reaching its limits, causing data congestion and unreliable connections.
- **Inefficient Automation:** Slow communication between robots and systems hindered the automation processes, affecting productivity and reducing the speed at which products were manufactured.

Solution

To address these challenges, **Ericsson deployed a 5G-powered factory** in which **Ultra-Reliable Low-Latency Communication (URLLC)** was at the core of the solution. The 5G network enabled real-time, high-speed communication between every aspect of the factory floor, from **robots** and **conveyor belts** to **smart sensors** and **AI-driven control systems**. The factory was equipped with **5G-enabled IoT devices** and edge computing solutions to handle the massive data flows generated by its operations.

Key elements of the solution included:

- **Real-Time Communication:** 5G allowed the factory's **robots, automated vehicles, and systems** to communicate instantly, with **minimal latency**, making decisions in real-time based on sensory input.
- **Network Slicing:** Ericsson leveraged **private 5G networks** with **network slicing**, which provided dedicated bandwidth for the factory's devices. This ensured that all devices operated in parallel without impacting the overall network efficiency.
- **Edge Computing Integration:** Data was processed **locally** on edge servers, minimizing the delay caused by transmitting large volumes of data to the cloud. This approach facilitated **real-time analysis** and **decision-making**, which improved the responsiveness of the entire manufacturing process.

Benefits

- **Faster Production Cycles:** With the ability to communicate in **real-time**, production lines became more responsive, reducing cycle times and improving overall efficiency. The factory achieved a **50% faster production rate** due to the reduction in delays caused by network latency.
- **High Reliability and Zero Downtime:** By utilizing 5G's **reliable connectivity**, Ericsson ensured that the factory's operations had an **uptime rate of 99.99%**. The ability to

maintain stable, fast connections allowed machines to operate seamlessly without interruption.

- **Cost Efficiency:** With the **elimination of legacy wiring** and the ability to scale up operations easily through wireless systems, Ericsson significantly reduced maintenance costs associated with outdated systems. Additionally, network slicing provided a **customized solution** for factory operations, ensuring optimal performance without compromising security or efficiency.

- **Enhanced Automation:** With fast, low-latency communication between devices, the robots and AI systems could work together more effectively, resulting in **more precise automation** and fewer human interventions, which improved product quality and consistency.

Case Study 2: BMW's AI-Enabled Edge IIoT System

Current Challenges

BMW's vehicle production facilities are massive, generating vast amounts of data from various machines, sensors, and robots. In the past, much of this data was sent to the cloud for analysis, but the amount of data generated was so large that the **latency of cloud computing** caused delays in decision-making. This slow response time was particularly problematic in high-speed environments like assembly lines, where quick adjustments to machine operations are critical for maintaining productivity.

The challenges faced by BMW before implementing an AI-enabled Edge IIoT system included:

- **Cloud-Processing Latency:** Cloud computing was often too slow to analyze the real-time data coming from machines. Delays in machine learning model updates resulted in inefficiencies and slowdowns on the production floor.

- **Inability to Handle Massive Data Volumes:** The sheer volume of data generated by sensors and robots required significant computational power, which was not feasible with cloud-only solutions.
- **Real-Time Decision-Making Issues:** Without timely insights, the factory's robots couldn't make adjustments to the production process in real-time, causing errors in product quality and inefficiencies.

Solution

To overcome these challenges, BMW implemented **AI-enabled Edge computing** within their production system. Edge devices were deployed to **process data locally**, instead of relying on a central cloud server. This enabled BMW to gain real-time insights from their machines without latency issues.

The solution included:

- **Edge AI Processing:** BMW's factory deployed **edge devices** to handle data processing locally on the factory floor. This **real-time data analysis** allowed for faster machine learning model updates, resulting in **immediate feedback** and improved manufacturing processes.
- **Connected Sensors and Machines:** The factory's **AI-driven robots** and **IoT sensors** communicated seamlessly over a **5G network**, providing real-time data updates on equipment performance.
- **Predictive Maintenance:** Using AI algorithms, the system analyzed data for signs of wear and tear on the machines, predicting when maintenance was required and preventing unexpected breakdowns.

Benefits

- **30% Improvement in Defect Detection:** With edge computing, BMW achieved faster analysis of sensor data, allowing for **quicker identification** and **rectification of defects** on the production line. This resulted in a 30%

improvement in detecting defects earlier in the process, reducing waste and increasing product quality.

- **Enhanced Predictive Maintenance:** The AI system's ability to predict equipment failures before they occurred resulted in a significant decrease in **unplanned downtime**, improving the reliability of machines and reducing maintenance costs.
- **Faster Decision-Making:** By processing data locally at the edge, BMW's factory reduced delays caused by cloud processing. This meant that robots and machines could adjust their actions **immediately** based on real-time data, improving the overall efficiency of the production process.
- **Optimized Production Line Operations:** With immediate access to **machine performance data**, BMW was able to continuously adjust operations, ensuring that robots were always functioning at optimal capacity and **maximizing productivity**.

Case Study 3: Tesla's Blockchain-Based Supply Chain

Current Challenges

Tesla's electric vehicle (EV) manufacturing relies heavily on the supply of specific raw materials, such as **lithium and cobalt**, for their batteries. However, **sourcing these materials** has always been a challenge due to the lack of transparency in the supply chain. Tesla faced difficulties in verifying the origin of materials, ensuring they were sourced sustainably, and confirming that suppliers were adhering to ethical labor standards.

Other challenges included:

- **Supply Chain Transparency:** Difficulty in verifying whether the materials used in production were sourced from **sustainable suppliers** and met **ethical standards**.
- **Traceability Issues:** With many suppliers involved, it was hard to track every **component and material** from **sourcing to delivery**.

- **Complex Regulatory Compliance:** Tesla had to comply with various **global regulations**, particularly regarding **ethical sourcing** and **environmental sustainability**.

Solution

To address these issues, Tesla implemented a **blockchain-based supply chain solution**. By leveraging blockchain, Tesla was able to create a **secure, transparent ledger** that tracked each **component** and **material** used in its vehicles from the point of origin to final assembly.

Key elements of the solution included:

- **Blockchain for Transparent Transactions:** Blockchain technology provided an immutable, tamper-proof ledger that recorded every **transaction** in the supply chain. This ensured that Tesla could trace the origin of all materials used in manufacturing.
- **Smart Contracts for Automatic Verification:** Tesla used **smart contracts** to automate the process of verifying supplier commitments to ethical sourcing and sustainability. These contracts ensured that each supplier adhered to the agreed terms before proceeding with material shipments.
- **Real-Time Supply Chain Visibility:** Tesla utilized blockchain to provide real-time data on the status and location of every material, from the **raw material stage** through to final product assembly.

Benefits

- **100% Transparency in the Supply Chain:** Tesla gained complete visibility into the source of every material used in their vehicles, providing customers and regulators with proof that their products were ethically sourced and environmentally sustainable.
- **Enhanced Compliance:** With blockchain's **automated record-keeping**, Tesla was able to easily meet **global regulations** regarding **ethical sourcing** and

environmental standards, avoiding fines and reputational risks.

- **Increased Customer Trust:** The transparency provided by blockchain helped **boost customer confidence** in Tesla's commitment to sustainability and ethical business practices.
- **Improved Efficiency in the Supply Chain:** The use of **smart contracts** automated the verification of supplier compliance, reducing delays and human intervention. This allowed Tesla to maintain a **faster, more reliable supply chain** while ensuring ethical and sustainable practices.

In conclusion, **Cyber-Physical Systems** provide the backbone for a fully connected and automated factory environment, ensuring real-time coordination, predictive maintenance, and efficient operations. By enabling seamless communication and synchronization between physical and digital systems, CPS creates the foundation for the **smart factory** of the future.

Trend #5: The Future Workforce in an Automated World

As we move deeper into the era of automation, it is inevitable that the future workforce will undergo significant transformations. The rapid advancements in technologies such as artificial intelligence (AI), robotics, and automation are reshaping industries across the globe, bringing both opportunities and challenges. The landscape of work is shifting, and with it, the roles, skill sets, and expectations of workers are evolving. By 2030, automation technologies will not only change the types of jobs available but also redefine the relationship between humans and machines in the workplace. While automation promises increased productivity and cost-efficiency, it also raises critical questions about job displacement, the future of labor, and the need for reskilling and upskilling. The balance between humans and machines will be critical in shaping a future workforce that is adaptable, skilled, and resilient in the face of disruptive changes.

6.1 How AI, Robotics, and Automation Will Reshape Jobs by 2030

The integration of **AI, robotics, and automation** into the workplace is already impacting the structure of industries, and by 2030, these technologies are expected to further reshape the job market. Many tasks that were once performed manually or required significant human intervention will be automated, leading to the displacement of some jobs. Roles that involve repetitive, predictable tasks, such as assembly line work, data entry, and customer service, will be most vulnerable to automation. **AI-powered systems** can already perform these tasks more efficiently and accurately, eliminating the need for human workers in these roles. As robots and automated systems become more advanced, their capabilities will extend to more complex tasks, such as medical diagnostics, financial analysis, and even creative professions like design and content creation.

However, automation does not only signify job loss. It will also create new roles that require higher levels of specialization and expertise. With the rise of **smart factories**, **autonomous vehicles**, and **digital services**, the demand for workers skilled in programming, AI development, machine learning, data analytics, and cybersecurity will surge. The workforce will shift from manual labor to more knowledge-based, tech-driven jobs. In addition to technical roles, there will be a growing need for workers who can manage, maintain, and improve automated systems. As companies look to implement and optimize these technologies, **robotics engineers**, **AI specialists**, and **data scientists** will become indispensable in the workforce.

Moreover, automation will give rise to new industries and business models. For instance, as **AI algorithms** become more integrated into everyday processes, the demand for new forms of human-machine interaction and digital services will create specialized sectors. These new industries will require workers who can leverage automation for tasks like improving customer experiences, enhancing business analytics, and optimizing production processes. The role of human workers will shift toward **higher-level tasks** that machines cannot replicate, such as strategic decision-making, creative problem-solving, and emotional intelligence in customer relations.

6.2 The Need for Reskilling and Upskilling in the Digital Era

With automation transforming the nature of work, **reskilling** and **upskilling** have become essential for workers who wish to remain relevant and competitive in the job market. As certain jobs become obsolete due to automation, workers must adapt by acquiring new skills that are in demand. Reskilling refers to the process of learning new skills to transition into a completely different job, while upskilling focuses on enhancing existing skills to stay current in an evolving field. Both are critical for ensuring that workers can continue to find meaningful employment as automation disrupts traditional industries.

The growing demand for **digital literacy** and technical skills is one of the primary drivers for reskilling initiatives. As automation and AI technologies evolve, workers need to understand how these systems work and how to use them effectively. **Technical skills** like programming, AI programming, cloud computing, and data analytics will be necessary for workers in a range of fields, from manufacturing to healthcare. At the same time, **soft skills** like critical thinking, adaptability, and emotional intelligence will become increasingly important as they complement the technical capabilities of automated systems. The emphasis on human skills that machines cannot replicate will help workers remain essential contributors to their organizations.

Reskilling and upskilling programs are essential for both workers and employers. Governments, educational institutions, and businesses must invest in training programs that help workers navigate these transitions. These initiatives could include online learning platforms, apprenticeship programs, and partnerships between private companies and educational institutions to develop curriculums tailored to the needs of the future workforce. In regions where traditional industries are being disrupted, such as manufacturing hubs or areas reliant on fossil fuels, targeted reskilling programs will be crucial for avoiding widespread job displacement. As the workforce becomes more adaptable, industries can harness the benefits of automation while ensuring a smooth transition for displaced workers.

6.3 Human-Robot Collaboration: The Role of Augmented Workforce

One of the most exciting developments in the future of work is the rise of **human-robot collaboration**, where humans and robots work side by side to achieve tasks that neither could accomplish alone. Rather than replacing humans, robots will increasingly serve as **collaborative partners**, augmenting human capabilities and enabling workers to focus on more strategic, creative, and decision-making tasks. This collaboration will be particularly important in industries like manufacturing, logistics, healthcare, and agriculture, where robots can handle repetitive, high-precision tasks, and humans provide the creativity, adaptability, and emotional intelligence necessary for more complex challenges.

Collaborative robots, or **cobots**, are designed to work safely alongside human workers, complementing their strengths while performing the more dangerous, monotonous, or physically demanding tasks. For example, in a manufacturing setting, cobots can handle heavy lifting, repetitive assembly tasks, and quality control inspections, while human workers oversee the process, troubleshoot problems, and perform tasks that require dexterity or decision-making. This type of collaboration not only improves efficiency and reduces the risk of injury but also enables workers to leverage the strengths of both humans and machines.

The concept of the **augmented workforce** extends beyond just robots. It encompasses a wide range of advanced technologies that enhance human performance, including **AI assistants**, **wearable devices**, and **augmented reality (AR)** tools. For instance, an AI-powered assistant could provide real-time data and insights to a worker on the factory floor, helping them make decisions more quickly and accurately. Similarly, AR devices can overlay digital information onto the physical world, assisting workers in complex assembly or maintenance tasks. In healthcare, robots can assist surgeons in performing delicate procedures with greater precision, while nurses and doctors provide the empathy and human touch that are essential to patient care.

Ultimately, the future workforce will not be defined by a conflict between humans and machines but by their **synergy**. As workers adapt to working alongside robots and AI systems, they will be able to accomplish more than ever before, combining the best of human ingenuity with the efficiency and precision of machines.

As automation and AI technologies reshape the workforce, ethical considerations will play a crucial role in ensuring that the transition is equitable and inclusive. The rapid pace of automation raises concerns about **job displacement, income inequality**, and **social disruption**. Without proper planning and intervention, automation could disproportionately affect low-wage workers, marginalized groups, and regions reliant on traditional industries. Ethical questions also arise around the responsibility of companies and governments in managing this transition and ensuring that workers are not left behind.

To address these concerns, governments and organizations must implement **policy interventions** that ensure the fair distribution of the benefits of automation. **Universal basic income (UBI)**, **portable benefits**, and **social safety nets** could provide a cushion for workers who lose their jobs due to automation. Additionally, policies aimed at supporting **small businesses** and **entrepreneurs** can help create new opportunities for employment and economic growth. Governments will need to play a central role in facilitating the transition by providing financial support for **reskilling programs**, offering incentives for companies to invest in **human-centric technologies**, and fostering an environment of innovation that includes a broad range of stakeholders.

Another ethical concern is the role of **AI decision-making** in the workplace. As AI systems become more involved in hiring, promotions, and performance evaluations, it is important to ensure that these systems are designed to be **fair**, **transparent**, and **accountable**. Biases in AI algorithms could perpetuate existing inequalities and lead to discrimination in hiring or job assignments. Establishing regulatory frameworks and industry standards for AI ethics will be critical in preventing these issues and ensuring that automation is implemented in a way that benefits society as a whole.

In conclusion, the future workforce in an automated world will require thoughtful consideration of ethical implications and a coordinated effort from governments, businesses, and workers to ensure a smooth and fair transition. By prioritizing **reskilling**, embracing **human-robot collaboration**, and implementing policies that address the social and ethical challenges of automation, society can unlock the full potential of these technologies while safeguarding the welfare of all workers.

6.5 Real-World Case Studies for the Future Workforce in an Automated World

The future of the workforce in an automated world is not a hypothetical scenario; it is already being shaped by real-world examples across various industries. Companies around the globe are implementing AI, robotics, and automation technologies to improve productivity, enhance worker safety, and foster new job roles. Below are five case studies illustrating how automation and AI are reshaping the workforce, the challenges companies face, the solutions they have implemented, and the benefits that have resulted.

Case Study 1: ABB's Collaborative Robots in Manufacturing

Current Challenges: ABB, a global leader in automation and robotics, operates several manufacturing plants worldwide. One significant challenge faced by ABB's manufacturing plants was the need to enhance production efficiency while reducing workplace injuries. The repetitive and physically demanding tasks, such as lifting and handling heavy parts, were particularly taxing on human workers. These tasks also led to high rates of workplace injuries, which affected employee morale and productivity.

Solution: ABB introduced collaborative robots, or **cobots**, into their manufacturing processes to assist human workers with heavy lifting, precision tasks, and assembly. These cobots are designed to work side by side with human operators in a safe and efficient manner. For example, a cobot might perform repetitive tasks like assembling parts or lifting components, while the human worker focuses on quality control, troubleshooting, and decision-making. The robots were equipped with advanced sensors and AI algorithms to ensure they could adapt to their environment and avoid accidents.

Benefits: The introduction of cobots helped ABB reduce the number of workplace injuries significantly, improving worker safety and satisfaction. Additionally, the cobots enhanced overall efficiency by performing tasks more quickly and accurately than humans. This collaboration allowed human workers to focus on more complex tasks, thus improving productivity. ABB also reported lower operational costs due to fewer workplace injuries and reduced downtime, highlighting the economic benefits of human-robot collaboration. The initiative also helped the company bridge the skills gap by allowing workers to transition into roles that require higher-level decision-making and technical skills.

Case Study 2: Amazon's Use of Robotics in Fulfillment Centers

Current Challenges: Amazon operates one of the largest fulfillment center networks globally, handling millions of orders daily. One of the biggest challenges Amazon faced was the need to meet growing demand while maintaining a high level of operational efficiency. Traditional methods of human labor were becoming increasingly inefficient as order volumes surged. Additionally, fulfillment centers required high staffing levels, leading to challenges in hiring and managing a large workforce. Human workers were also susceptible to fatigue and injury due to the physically demanding nature of the tasks.

Solution: Amazon deployed a fleet of robots, including the **Kiva robots**, to assist with product picking, packing, and sorting. These robots are designed to move shelves of products around the warehouse to human workers, who then pick the items for orders. The robots use AI algorithms to optimize their movements, ensuring the most efficient routes for picking and reducing the time spent on each task. The robots work alongside human workers, enhancing their productivity while reducing the physical strain on them.

Benefits: The implementation of robotics in Amazon's fulfillment centers resulted in a significant boost in productivity. The robots reduced the time it took to process each order, leading to faster delivery times and increased order fulfillment capacity. This allowed Amazon to meet growing consumer demand without the need to hire additional workers at the same rate. Furthermore, human workers were able to focus on more complex tasks that robots could not handle, such as quality checks and customer service. The use of robotics also led to a safer work environment by reducing physical strain and the risk of injury among employees. As a result, Amazon reported improved worker satisfaction and lower injury rates, along with a boost in overall profitability.

Case Study 3: Siemens' Digital Workforce in Smart Factories

Current Challenges: Siemens, a global technology company, has been at the forefront of advancing digital technologies in industrial settings. One of the challenges Siemens faced was the inefficiency of traditional factory operations, which relied heavily on human labor and were prone to errors and delays. Additionally, Siemens had to address the skills gap in its workforce, particularly in manufacturing roles that required specialized technical knowledge. Traditional training methods were not sufficient to equip workers with the advanced skills needed to operate complex digital and automation systems.

Solution: Siemens implemented a **digital workforce** solution by integrating AI, IoT, and robotics into its smart factories. The company introduced **AI-powered tools** for workers, such as virtual assistants and real-time data analytics, to help them make faster and more informed decisions. They also introduced **augmented reality (AR)** for training and on-the-job guidance. The use of AR allowed workers to receive step-by-step instructions while interacting with machinery, which enhanced their ability to perform complex tasks. Siemens also created a platform for reskilling and upskilling, enabling workers to acquire the necessary skills to work with these advanced technologies.

Benefits: Siemens' smart factory approach led to significant improvements in operational efficiency and product quality. The AI-powered systems allowed for real-time monitoring and adjustments to the production line, resulting in reduced downtime and fewer errors. The integration of AR into training programs accelerated the learning curve for workers, allowing them to quickly adapt to the new digital tools. Furthermore, the reskilling programs helped bridge the skills gap, ensuring that workers could remain relevant in an increasingly automated world. Siemens also reported higher employee satisfaction and engagement due to the opportunities for growth and development provided by the digital workforce.

Case Study 4: Universal Robots and Human-Robot Collaboration in the Electronics Industry

Current Challenges: The electronics industry faces intense pressure to meet rising demand for high-quality products at a faster pace. However, many of the tasks in the production process, such as component placement and testing, are highly repetitive and prone to human error. In addition, the industry is facing a shortage of skilled labor, particularly in regions with high demand for electronics. The challenge was to find a solution that could maintain production quality while addressing the labor shortage and improving productivity.

Solution: Universal Robots, a leading provider of collaborative robotics, introduced **cobots** to assist with the repetitive tasks in electronics manufacturing. These robots were deployed to work alongside human operators, handling tasks such as placing components on circuit boards, testing products, and packaging. The cobots are easy to program and adapt to different tasks, allowing for quick adjustments when product designs change. The robots were also integrated with **AI-powered vision systems** to detect defects in real-time, ensuring high-quality production.

Benefits: The deployment of cobots in electronics manufacturing led to significant improvements in both efficiency and product quality. The robots were able to perform repetitive tasks with greater accuracy and speed than human workers, reducing production errors and improving overall throughput. Additionally, by automating routine tasks, workers were freed up to focus on higher-value activities, such as quality control and process optimization. The use of cobots also helped address the labor shortage by allowing companies to scale their production without the need for a larger workforce. As a result, manufacturers saw a reduction in labor costs and a boost in overall profitability.

Case Study 5: L'Oréal's Virtual Reality and AI-Driven Retail Experience

Current Challenges: L'Oréal, one of the world's leading cosmetics companies, faced a challenge in its retail operations as the industry shifted toward more personalized and tech-driven customer experiences. Traditional retail models, which relied on human sales associates to recommend products, were becoming outdated in the face of growing demand for online shopping and digital engagement. L'Oréal needed a solution that could enhance the in-store customer experience while maintaining the personal touch that consumers value.

Solution: L'Oréal implemented **virtual reality (VR)** and **AI-driven technologies** to transform its retail operations. In collaboration with various retail partners, L'Oréal introduced AI-powered virtual assistants to provide personalized product recommendations to customers. These AI systems were integrated into a VR platform, allowing customers to experience products virtually before making a purchase. The company also introduced AI tools that could analyze customer preferences and provide customized beauty solutions in real-time. The use of AI-driven chatbots and virtual consultations allowed customers to interact with L'Oréal's products from the comfort of their homes.

Benefits: The integration of VR and AI in retail allowed L'Oréal to enhance the customer experience by providing personalized and immersive shopping options. The use of AI-driven virtual assistants improved the efficiency and accuracy of product recommendations, which increased customer satisfaction and loyalty. By offering virtual consultations, L'Oréal was able to reach a broader customer base and cater to the growing demand for digital engagement in the beauty industry. This innovation led to increased sales and a more efficient use of human resources, as retail staff could focus on more complex customer interactions while AI and VR handled routine inquiries and recommendations.

These case studies demonstrate how automation and AI are reshaping industries and the workforce, addressing challenges such as labor shortages, inefficiencies, and the need for reskilling. As companies continue to embrace these technologies, the future workforce will be increasingly defined by human-robot collaboration, the integration of AI, and a focus on continuous learning and adaptability. The benefits of these transformations will not only be seen in productivity improvements but also in worker safety, job satisfaction, and new opportunities for career growth.

Conclusion: The Road Ahead

As we look ahead to the next decade in industrial automation, we are standing at a pivotal moment in the evolution of technology and manufacturing. The trends and innovations we have discussed throughout this book — ranging from the integration of AI, robotics, and the Industrial Internet of Things (IIoT) to the deployment of 5G, edge computing, blockchain, and cybersecurity advancements — will be key drivers in reshaping industries across the globe. However, these transformations come with both opportunities and challenges that must be carefully navigated. The future of industrial automation is not just about the technologies themselves, but about how businesses, governments, and workers collaborate to create a sustainable, productive, and inclusive industrial ecosystem.

7.1 Predicting the Next Decade in Industrial Automation

Looking to the future, one of the most exciting aspects of industrial automation is its potential to unlock new levels of efficiency and innovation across diverse sectors. In the next decade, we will likely see several key trends emerge as dominant forces in shaping the industrial landscape.

One major trend is the continued integration of AI and machine learning into industrial systems. AI will become more pervasive, driving not just automation in manufacturing lines but also enhancing predictive analytics, quality control, and decision-making across the entire production lifecycle. With deeper integration, AI-powered systems will be able to optimize production processes in real time, predict machine failures before they occur, and suggest improvements for efficiency that are far beyond human capabilities. Over time, these systems will evolve into intelligent factories, capable of making autonomous decisions based on real-time data from across the supply chain.

The rise of collaborative robots (cobots) will be another significant trend in industrial automation. These robots, which work alongside human operators rather than replacing them, are expected to play a vital role in reducing workplace injuries, increasing productivity, and improving the flexibility of production lines. With advances in AI and robotics, cobots will become increasingly adaptive, able to handle more complex tasks that were previously considered too difficult for machines. This will allow for the development of more dynamic and flexible manufacturing environments, where robots and humans work together seamlessly.

Edge computing will also see substantial growth as manufacturers continue to move towards decentralized processing to reduce latency and improve real-time data analysis. As more sensors, devices, and machines are connected through IIoT, the need for processing data closer to the source will become increasingly important. Edge computing will facilitate quicker decision-making, enabling faster reactions to issues like equipment malfunctions or production bottlenecks. This will help drive greater efficiency and resilience in industrial operations.

5G technology is another critical component in this next wave of industrial automation. The ability to deliver ultra-reliable low-latency communication will unlock real-time data transfer for connected devices in factories, helping to improve coordination across machine-to-machine and machine-to-human interactions. This will enable manufacturers to run more agile and flexible production lines, as 5G networks allow devices and machines to operate more effectively in a highly connected environment. As a result, we expect to see widespread adoption of 5G in smart factories, transportation, logistics, and beyond.

In addition, sustainability will become a central theme in the next decade of industrial automation. As pressure mounts from governments and the public to reduce carbon footprints, industries will need to adopt energy-efficient automation solutions that minimize waste and improve resource management. We are already seeing automation being used in green energy technologies, such as solar power, wind energy, and electric vehicles, and this trend is set to accelerate. Over the next ten years, the convergence of automation and sustainability will lead to smarter energy systems, optimized waste management, and more eco-friendly industrial processes.

Lastly, workforce transformation will continue to be a defining factor in the future of industrial automation. As AI and automation technologies evolve, the workforce will increasingly need to reskill and upskill in order to thrive in this new environment. This will require a comprehensive approach to workforce development, one that includes retraining workers for new roles in AI, data analysis, and robotics, as well as fostering lifelong learning opportunities to ensure a steady supply of skilled labor in the future.

7.2 The Role of Governments and Industry Leaders in Automation Growth

The role of governments and industry leaders in the advancement of industrial automation cannot be overstated. While technology development and adoption will primarily be driven by the private sector, governments and policymakers will play a crucial role in ensuring that these advances are leveraged for the benefit of society as a whole. This includes addressing key issues such as labor displacement, data security, intellectual property rights, and environmental impact.

Governments must first acknowledge the potential of automation to drive economic growth and innovation, while also recognizing the need for thoughtful regulation. This will involve the creation of policies that encourage innovation while managing the challenges that automation brings, such as job displacement and the widening skills gap. A critical aspect of this will be creating incentives for companies to invest in workforce retraining and reskilling programs, ensuring that displaced workers can transition into new roles created by automation. Governments will also need to prioritize investment in infrastructure, including the rollout of 5G networks, edge computing, and IoT, to enable seamless connectivity in industrial environments.

Industry leaders, on the other hand, will need to embrace a forward-thinking mindset, not just in terms of implementing new technologies but also in considering their social and environmental implications. Leading companies will be the ones that take a holistic approach to automation, ensuring that it is not just about efficiency and cost reduction, but also about improving quality of life for workers, reducing environmental impact, and contributing to the broader social good.

Industry leaders must also collaborate across sectors to share knowledge and best practices, which will help accelerate the adoption of automation and ensure its benefits are widely distributed. Companies that are at the forefront of automation will have the opportunity to set the standards for the industry, influencing everything from safety regulations to ethical AI development.

7.3 Key Challenges and Opportunities in Adopting These Trends

While the opportunities in industrial automation are vast, there are several challenges that must be addressed to ensure successful adoption and integration. One of the biggest challenges is workforce displacement. As automation technologies such as robotics and AI are integrated into manufacturing processes, the need for certain types of human labor will diminish. For example, routine manual labor tasks may be replaced by machines, while higher-level decision-making may be automated through AI algorithms. This creates significant challenges for workers who may not have the skills necessary to transition into more advanced roles.

The key opportunity here lies in reskilling and upskilling the workforce. If workers are given access to training programs that teach the skills required for the jobs of the future, they can not only transition smoothly into new roles but also help accelerate the adoption of automation technologies. In this sense, automation can create new opportunities for workers rather than simply taking them away.

Another significant challenge in the adoption of industrial automation is data security. With the increase in connectivity through IIoT, cloud computing, and edge devices, there are growing concerns about the vulnerability of industrial systems to cyberattacks. Industrial sectors are prime targets for cybercriminals, and a breach in security could have catastrophic consequences, including system failures, production delays, and loss of proprietary data.

However, the opportunity here lies in the development of cybersecurity solutions that are specifically tailored for industrial automation environments. As companies integrate AI and IoT into their operations, they will need to prioritize the development of robust cybersecurity measures to protect both their data and the infrastructure they rely on. This includes adopting end-to-end encryption, implementing multi-factor authentication, and employing advanced AI systems to monitor for threats in real time.

Another challenge is the cost and complexity of implementation. While the long-term benefits of automation are clear, the upfront costs associated with integrating new technologies into existing infrastructure can be prohibitively high for some companies. The complexity of integrating AI, robotics, IoT, and other technologies into existing production lines can also be a significant hurdle for many organizations.

However, this challenge presents an opportunity for innovative financing models and new approaches to technology integration. Companies can explore partnerships, subsidies, or government grants to offset initial investment costs. Moreover, the rise of modular automation systems and cloud-based solutions is making it easier for companies of all sizes to adopt automation technologies at a manageable scale, reducing both financial and operational barriers to entry.

Lastly, ethics and policy around the use of automation, particularly AI, are significant concerns. The automation of decision-making processes, especially when it comes to critical applications like healthcare, finance, and manufacturing, raises questions about accountability and transparency. How do we ensure that AI systems are not making biased or harmful decisions? How can we trust autonomous systems to act in the best interests of society?

The opportunity here lies in the development of ethical frameworks for AI and automation technologies. Governments and industry leaders must work together to establish standards for responsible AI usage, ensuring that automated systems are fair, transparent, and accountable. By establishing strong ethical guidelines, we can create a future where automation not only improves efficiency and productivity but also benefits society in a positive and equitable manner.

7.4 Final Thoughts and Call to Action

The road ahead for industrial automation is filled with incredible potential, but it also requires careful consideration and responsible action. The technologies that are shaping the future of manufacturing and production have the power to transform industries, boost economies, and improve the lives of workers around the globe. However, the successful adoption of these technologies will depend on how we manage the challenges associated with them, from workforce displacement to cybersecurity concerns.

As we move into the next decade, it is essential that governments, industry leaders, and workers collaborate to ensure that the benefits of automation are widely distributed. This will require investment in training and education, strong ethical frameworks, and a commitment to sustainable and inclusive growth. Industry leaders must embrace innovation while also prioritizing the well-being of their workers, ensuring that automation is not a force of disruption but a tool for creating new opportunities.

The next decade of industrial automation is not just about technology — it's about people. It's about enabling workers to thrive in an increasingly automated world, about ensuring that automation benefits all stakeholders, and about creating a future where technology enhances human potential rather than replaces it. The future of industrial automation is bright, and the road ahead is one we must walk together. Let's take action now to shape that future for the better.